ABOVE
THE STORM

CAROPSON

ii

TABLE OF CONTENTS

iv

PREFACE

This book is about eagles, God's principles for life, and my grandchildren. It may seem like an unlikely combination, but God is the One who gave me the ideas and brought this book together, and so I trust Him to use it for His glory.

This book is not intended to be a scientific study of eagles. I have gathered the information from over 25 years of studying eagles, hearing stories about them and even observing them myself, but I am not an expert nor a scientist. However, as I've used these eagle illustrations to share God's truths over the years, I've been asked repeatedly to write them down for others to enjoy and share. So, after much prayer, the Lord has led me to write what I've learned in a devotional form.

The reason for my interest in eagles is two-fold. First of all, I noticed that God used eagles in His Word to illustrate various truths He wanted to teach us.

For instance, the title of this book comes from learning what Isaiah 40:31 means when it says:

Those who wait for the Lord will gain new strength; they will mount up with wings like eagles, they will run and not get tired, they will walk and not become weary.

In these pages you will learn what it means to "mount up with wings as eagles" and rise "above the storm" in your daily life. You will also learn the meaning of Exodus 19:4 where God tells us, "You yourselves have seen what I did to the Egyptians, and how I bore you on eagles' wings, and brought you to Myself." As I've learned the meaning of these verses, it has helped me understand God's incredible love and provision for me in a deeper way.

My second reason for studying eagles is related to starting a Christian school twenty-five years ago. When my husband and I sat in our living room and thought about what mascot we'd like for our new school, we decided on the eagle. We then wanted to be able to teach our young students what it would mean to be an "eagle Christian," and so my study began. I wanted to learn how to relate to them the truths of God's word in a way that they could easily remember and understand, and so God began giving me the eagle illustrations you will see in this book. They have grown and developed over the years due to God's working in my life.

As I share the eagle stories in my speaking, I also share many "Nana stories" about my grandchildren and am always asked if they are in my books. So, I've included one of these stories at the end of each chapter.

I pray that, as you read and remember the eagle illustrations, you will always be reminded of the truths of God's Word and their importance and power in your life. Then, I pray that you will find that Jesus is your source of strength, and He is the only One who can and will enable you to rise "above the storms" that you face each day. As with each of my previous books, I ask God to use these pages to uplift you, encourage you, and draw you closer to Himself.

All the praise goes to my Heavenly Father for what He accomplishes in your heart and life as you read this book.

Written with love for my Savior
Carol Hopson

CHAPTER 1 | DAILY SURVIVAL

Do you feel like Satan is on the attack morning and evening? Do you wake up with the same concerns that you went to bed with? Are you feeling weighted down with worries before your day even begins? I've been there too! You've prayed and read the Word and still you battle discouragement and fear all day long.

In forty years of ministry, my husband and I have had to handle many times of discouragement, frustration, anxiety, and brokenness. But, through those difficult days, we learned something about the eagle's daily preparation that helped us discover the peace God desires to give us each day. The eagle begins each day with a special process called preening. He spends about an hour each morning passing each feather through his beak to "steam clean" it for the day, because he knows how important this morning routine is.

A mature eagle has about 7,000 feathers which are made of keratin, like our hair and nails. These feathers consist of interlocking microscopic structures that are light, but very strong. The layers of feathers trap the air to insulate the bird against the cold and protect it from the rain. However, the preening process is how he protects and cares for these feathers. So, after "steam cleaning" each one through his beak, he releases a chemical from his preening gland that waterproofs the feathers to protect them against storms, mud, mirky water, or whatever he faces in his search for food. This then, is his daily preparation.

As I discovered this about the eagle, the Lord opened my eyes to what my daily routine should be, especially during times of discouragement, weariness, or doubt. My husband and I began a "preening" process each morning in our devotional time. We would steam clean our lives by asking forgiveness first of all, for the doubts of the night, or yesterday's fears. We would make sure that our hearts were clean before we began the day.

Create in me a clean heart, Oh God, and renew a steadfast spirit within me.

(Psalm 51:10)

I found it impossible to be steadfast in my faith if I didn't have a clean heart, and so this cleansing time was extremely important. I think that so often we overlook our own sin and try to go on with our lives, expecting God to bless us. Some of the sins that seem to easily slip our minds are anger...a bitter thought...a critical spirit...an unforgiving heart...a judgmental attitude...a worried mind. When any of these are present, we are soiled and not ready to handle the battles of the day.

The second part of our daily preparation would be to "waterproof" ourselves by taking a Scripture verse to commit to memory for the day. We would then use it to defeat Satan's attacks as they came thoughout our days. When attacked with thoughts such as, "This problem isn't going away and your ministry is going to suffer greatly," we would recite *"He who began a good work in you will perform it until the day of Jesus Christ."* (Philippians 1:6)

When faced with fear about our future we'd recall:

Do not fear, for I am with you. Do not anxiously look about you, for I am your God. I will strengthen you; surely I will help you. Surely I will uphold you with my righteous right hand.
(Isaiah 41:10)

This preening process became precious to us and helped us stay faithful during a very difficult time in our lives. Another way we prepare in the morning is to use the following acrostic:

P - praise
R - repent
A – ask
Y – yield

When speaking, I often ask women if they would ever consider getting up and going about their day, feeding their children, going to the store etc., without putting any clothes on. Of course, they look at me with horror and shake their heads, letting me know that I've gone a little insane. Then I share with them that we often go through our day, totally unclothed spiritually. Colossians 3:12-17 tells us we are to be "clothed" with compassion, kindness, humility, gentleness and patience. I then ask them to try spending five to ten minutes each morning, before facing their family or their day, getting "spiritually clothed." Here is how the acrostic I've shared above clothes me for the day.

In my "praise" time, I try to praise God for His attributes, His faithfulness, His forgiveness, His plan for me, His abundant love, the specific blessings He has poured on me and my family. As I move on to "repentance," I have to reflect on times that I went against what God's Word says and then confess it. Maybe I awoke in the night with some doubts. Maybe I held a grudge against my husband. God always brings to mind something for which I need to be cleansed. And when my heart is cleansed, my relationship with my Savior is restored and I'm ready to hear Him lead me throughout the day.

The "ask" part of the prayer is where I lay down my load. I tell God about all the things that are on my heart, things I want to change but can't. I pray for loved ones and ask for specific things for each one. I take whatever concerns me and leave it at Jesus' feet. Then I can go on about my day with a free spirit that's ready to love and forgive others. I'm ready to look for ways to serve the Lord because I'm not consumed with my own circumstances or worries.

The final preparation is to "yield" myself and my day to the Lord. This is when I pray, "Lord, I accept whatever You put into or take out of my life today. Please help me trust You and use all that today brings for your glory." When I've started my day with this prayer, I don't become discouraged or overwhelmed with circumstances that I didn't plan on because I've already committed them to the Lord. And, I remember that I've given Him full control of my day, so whatever I'm facing is not a surprise to Him. Therefore I can relax and rest and go with His plan.

Last week, I had a very busy speaking schedule and was traveling to early morning meetings two days in a row. On both mornings, there was an accident on the road which caused almost an hour delay each morning. This can be extremely frustrating for a speaker who always likes to be early, or at least very prompt. So, situations like this can make me tense, nervous, worried, and frustrated. I had been given no cell number so couldn't contact anyone to let them know where I was. Now here's the exciting part! As I came to a dead stand-still in the traffic, the Holy Spirit immediately recalled to my mind the prayer I had made that morning. I remembered that I had yielded my plans to God's plans and asked Him to help me use it for His glory. This was not a surprise to God! This was out of my control but not out of His. And so, I completely relaxed in my Heavenly Father's presence and spent the time loving Him and praising Him and thanking Him for whatever He was going to do. Believe me, this is not my human response to a traffic delay and not being on time for a speaking engagement. But God, in His grace, helped me go with His plan.

On both mornings, at different places, God rearranged the schedules so that this wasn't a problem for them. And, as I shared with the women of my delay and what God had done in my heart, it truly touched others. I had many women tell me that it was just what they needed to hear and the illustration was so fresh, personal, and real that they could understand and identify with it. Thank you, God, for teaching me this precious truth.

Come to me all who are weary and heavy-laden and I will give you rest. Take My yoke upon you, and learn from Me, for I am gentle and humble in heart; and you shall find rest for your souls. For My yoke is easy, and My load is light.

(Matthew 11:28-30)

NANA'S STORY

Little Jack was visiting us and we loved having him and his big brother, Elliot, come and spend the night with us. I usually tried to get up a little earlier than the boys so I could be ready for the day before they needed my attention. This particular morning, Jack came sleepily into the bathroom where I was putting my makeup on. He rubbed his eyes and said, "Morning, Nana." I knelt down, hugged him and responded, "Morning, Jack." I then returned to finish the task at hand. I was using my eyelash curler while Jack looked up at me and said, "Nana, what you doing?" To which I replied, "I'm putting my makeup on, Jack."

Jack studied me for another minute or two and then asked, "Nana, why for you do that?" Of course, I answered brilliantly, "It's supposed to make Nana look pretty." That's when my precious grandson thoughtfully replied, "Nana, I don't sink it's working!"

If we say that we have no sin, we are deceiving ourselves, and the truth is not in us. If we confess our sins, He is faithful and righteous to forgive us our sins and to cleanse us from all urighteousness."

(1 John 1:8,9)

Have you tried hard to make something work in your own strength, but to no avail? Maybe you need to do some spiritual preening today.

TO PREEN OR NOT TO PREEN

To preen, or not to preen?
The question of the day
Should I just go on with life
Assuming I'm okay?

Should I stop and clean my heart
Before my day begins?
Or should I just get going with
My work that never ends?

Is there time to read a verse
And all my sins confess?
Is there time to pray that God
Will free me of my stress?

If there's not time to talk with God
Before I hit the road
Then I must realize my life
Will be a heavy load.

Carol Hopson

CHAPTER 2

WHEN THE ENEMY APPROACHES

I've seen it happen over and over again. I've been sitting with a woman and I've heard such anger and bitterness come out of her mouth. One woman in particular comes to mind. Because of her husband's work, they had moved to San Diego from another state and she hated it, not because it was a terrible place to live, but because it wasn't what she wanted. She had asked to meet with me and was now reciting her husband's faults and all of her problems. She didn't want to move, she didn't have family here, she had no friends, she didn't want to go to a new church, she didn't want to speak to her husband or show him any love, she hated his job, she couldn't stand her kids, and so on. Yet, this person claimed to be a Christian who loved the Lord and wanted to please Him. How could anyone get so off track? How could such anger and resentment take hold in a believer's life? Doesn't God promise that *"He will work all things together for good to them that love God and are called according to His purpose"*? (Romans 8:28) To help explain what had happened to her, I need to tell you what the eagle must constantly be on the lookout for.

Because the eagle makes his nest so high up, he doesn't have to fear many predators. But there is one enemy that can be deadly to the baby eaglets if they are not protected by their parents. This enemy is the snake. He will seek to slither up the mountain, cliff, or tree and try to stay hidden until he appears in the nest. If the eaglets spot him, they will screech as loud as they can, which is a call for help from their mother. If she is close by, she will swoop in to rescue her young. She will either peck the snake to death right there or even bite his head completely off. Another way she might get rid of the enemy is to grab it with her strong talons and fly in search of a sharp rock or cliff and then throw it against the rock to kill it. In both instances, the attack on the enemy is immediate and successful. She doesn't wait to see what will happen, she is keenly aware of the danger and the enemy is not welcome in her home.

There are two things we can learn from this. The first is how sneaky the serpent is. It is hardly ever seen until it is ready to do great harm and I believe that it's the same in our spiritual lives. Satan can slither his way into our lives through our thoughts and emotions, if we're not alert and watching for danger.

Be of sober spirit, be on the alert. Your adversary, the devil, prowls about like a roaring lion seeking someone to devour. But resist him, firm in your faith...

(1 Peter 5:8,9a)

This woman had opened the door to anger and bitterness without even realizing that Satan had worked his way in and was "chewing her up." She was so deep into her own hurts and emotions, which is Satan's strategy, that she couldn't clearly see what damage she was doing to herself and her family, let alone the pain this was bringing to her Lord.

After listening to her, I asked her what she thought of God's Word. She replied that she believed it and thought we should obey it. I asked if she was willing to see what God's Word had to say about her situation. She seemed surprised, but said she was willing.

Then I turned to Philippians 4:4 which says:

Rejoice in the Lord always; and again I will say rejoice!

We then looked at Philippians 2:3-8 where God tells us to have the attitude that was in Christ Jesus, who did nothing from selfishness and didn't look out for his own interests, but the interests of others. Then He didn't demand His rights but emptied Himself, humbled Himself and was obedient even unto death. As we talked about this, the Holy Spirit began to work in her life to show her how selfish and self-centered she had become. We looked at other Scriptures to see where our true joy is found and she finally recognized how strangled she was by Satan's hold on her life. At this point she realized that she hadn't "killed the attacker" at the first approach and we went back to discover how it all began. She then realized that she had let a seed of bitterness take root in her heart and we talked of how it grew day by day. That little seed, allowed to flourish, had brought her to a point of hatred, anger, discontent, and had almost destroyed her marriage and home.

As she repented and committed to seek God's will for her life each day, her countenance began to change and the anger was gone. It was a few weeks later when her husband told me, with great joy, of the total change that was brought about in their family after that day. To God be the glory!

The second thing we learn from this eagle illustration is how quickly we need to recognize the enemy. We need to deal him and his work a deadly blow at first sight. For instance, when we feel the first seed of anger, bitterness, or resentment begin in our hearts, we need to go to God's Word and prayer immediately. The problem usually is that we don't recognize the first attack. This is why it's so important to read God's Word daily and pray, asking God to show us when we are off track.

Just this past week, God did just that for me. While preparing for a trip, my husband had offered to take things out of my briefcase and pack them into a larger case where we were combining our work in preparation for a plane flight. My thoughtful husband didn't want me to have to carry anything extra so he offered to put my things with his and he would carry it all. This included my laptop computer and made his bag very heavy. What a sweet, loving thing to do. However, as we got on the airplane, I asked for my computer and my folder of work. He reached into his overstuffed briefcase and pulled out my computer. He then searched for my folder, the one with all my research and work in it! He couldn't find it! Somehow, it hadn't been moved from my briefcase with the rest of the papers. I was not pleased! I was going to be away for a whole week and was planning to work very hard on this manuscript and my upcoming messages, but it was all in my folder...at home. My first thoughts were not about my loving husband and how he had tried to help me. They were very different from that. Then suddenly, I realized that this was Satan's attack on me and on our trip together. He did not want this to be a time of growth and sweet fellowship. He had planted the seed of anger and wanted it to grow. Praise God that it didn't and this trip turned out to be one of the most uplifting, nurturing, special times we had experienced in years.

The enemy will keep attacking, but we always have the choice to trust God, give up our will and accept God's plan and, in that way, totally defeat his plan. Then we need to thank God for loving us and ask Him to use us for His glory in this circumstance. I've often asked God, in my weakness, to shine a floodlight on my future. I wanted Him to let me know why I was facing a certain trial or at least show me how it was all going to turn out. Then I could be oh so faithful! But, that is not God's way.

He reminds me that:

His word is a lamp to my feet and a light to my path.

(Psalm 119:105)

He promises just enough light for the next step and wants me to trust Him with the rest. Satan loves to use the tools of doubt, fear, and discontent, but he is totally defeated by a trusting, thankful heart.

NANA'S STORY

We were in the final hour of our visit to LegoLand with Monica and Becca, our precious granddaughters. We had enjoyed a wonderful time and now Nana and Papa were going to buy each of them a little souvenir to take home with them. Three-year old Becca looked and looked through all the "stuff" and finally settled on a tiny Lego Flashlight keychain. It was about the smallest thing in the store but that was what Becca wanted and she was thrilled with it.

As soon as we arrived home, Becca wanted to shine her new treasure in the dark so I suggested that she go to our walk-in closet where it was dark. She ran in and, after a few minutes, she returned to get her big sister, Monica. She wanted to share her excitement with her so she called out, "Moni, come wif me! You don't need to be a...scared of the dark 'cause I have a lashlight." Now let me tell you that this was the tiniest "lashlight" I had ever seen, and the light that it gave in that big closet must have been a mere speck on the wall, but it was enough to remove Becca's fears.

As often happens, God spoke to me at that moment and said, "Carol, you don't need a spotlight, I have given you a "lashlight" for your path today. That's all you need.

The unfolding of Thy words gives light; it gives understanding to the simple.

(Psalm 119:130)

Why do I always think I need a spotlight? Because I'm not content to trust God's leading just one step at a time. I pray that I'm learning to take just one step at a time....for His glory!

JUST ONE STEP AT A TIME

Just one step at a time is all
my Savior wants from me.
He doesn't think I need to know
two years ahead or three.

He surely knows that I would faint
if I saw far ahead
I'd have to live in fear and doubt
and face each day with dread.

So in His knowing love for me
He works His plan divine.
Then gives me grace to follow Him
just one step at a time.

Carol Hopson

CHAPTER 3

COMFORT IN LONELINESS

I think most of us have had times when we were lonely. Maybe we were even surrounded by family or friends and we still felt lonely. My times of loneliness have come when God has asked me to move away from everything and everyone I loved. I had to leave my children, grandchildren, parents, and friends and start all over. I left our home, the sunshine, our ministries and life-long friends. God didn't ask me to do this once, but several times, and I learned what loneliness was really like. Before this, I always had lots of friends and was in the center of lots of activities. My father was the pastor of our church, and my husband was the Principal of the school, and so lots of people knew me and I had a huge network to draw from at any time. There was always a family member or friend to get together with whenever I desired it. There was always someone I could turn to for support or encouragement. But all of that changed when God moved us.

I was used to wearing many hats in my life. I was mother, wife, daughter, Bible teacher, mentor, friend, counselor, choir director, and speaker. But when I moved to a new state, no one knew about any of those hats. In fact, they didn't even know that I existed. Suddenly, I knew no one and no one knew me. What a shock! I knew that the move was God's will for my life and I knew He had a purpose which I couldn't yet see. But, the loneliness was still real to me. Who could I call to meet me for a cup of coffee? Who could I tell about my grandchild's latest stroke of genius? Who could I share a prayer request with?

It was during this time that God showed me one of the purposes of loneliness. I discovered that the only One I had to turn to was my Heavenly Father. I'd ask Him who I was now, and He'd lovingly remind me that I was His child, and that was enough. As I'd sit in my house, wondering what the day would bring, I discovered anew how precious it was to belong to Him and draw closer to Him. I spent my time talking with Him all day long as if He was my dearest friend who came to spend the week with me. Then I realized that this was exactly what He wanted to be.

Let me stop at this point and tell you about the lonely eagle. There is a long period before an eagle reaches maturity where he chooses to be all alone. During this time he will become a skilled hunter, will live alone, and have no nest of his own. He cannot be lured into joining other birds because he is steadfast in his preparation for the future. It is during this time that he learns how to handle the wind currents which we will discuss in a future chapter. He will live this way until he is ready to mate for life. As with other things in his life, the lonely years are years of preparation and maturity. They are extremely necessary for his future success. The lonely years of an eagle give him the experience and perspective that will last him the rest of his life.

Let's go back to my story. It was during those first lonely months, in a new place, that God showed me a new perspective. He revealed to me that He wanted me to open my eyes to others around me....anywhere....everywhere....and see their need and their loneliness. I no longer had a life filled with family, friends and ministry, but that was God's plan for me. He wanted to give me an experience that would change me forever...and it did. Words cannot express the joy I've found in taking God's love to people at the cleaners, the beauty salon, a restaurant, the Post Office, on a plane or train, or someone just sitting on a bench. (I've written about many of these stories in my book, *"My Day, His Way."*

Everywhere I went, God opened my eyes to people who were lonely or hurting, and I tried to bring them God's love and healing. Sometimes, it was a profound, life-changing meeting. Other times, it was a small hug from God for someone who was discouraged. One of those times was when I was simply going to the grocery store. I had prayed that God would make me available to see others through His eyes that day, but as I raced into the grocery store, I had already forgotten my prayer. As I began to fill my grocery cart, my thoughts kept going back to the young man outside the store who was trying to raise money for a Christian youth organization. I had been polite and even said, "God bless you" as I passed by him; but I kept thinking of the defeated look on his face as I walked in without stopping. With the prodding of the Holy Spirit, I returned the things in my cart and went back outside. I told the young man that I was a Christian and I was sorry that I walked right past him and then asked if he was discouraged, as he looked very sad and tired. He told me that it had been an awful day. No one was interested and no one was stopping to give to God's work and then he said these words, "I feel like a total failure for God."

Now I knew why God had been working on my heart. With a heart of love I took his hand and said, "Oh, you are definitely not a failure in God's eyes. In fact, you are bringing God great joy today!" He responded that he hadn't brought in any money all morning. "Do you think that's what God is interested in?" I asked. "He has all the resources in the world and He could fill that bucket in five seconds if He chose to." I went on to share with him that he was bringing joy to God just because he was willing and available. The rest was up to God. I reminded him that we are not responsible to bring in results, just to be available for God to use. Tears welled up in his eyes and he said, "I never thought of it that way." He thanked me for my time and I gave him a little hug and went on inside to begin my grocery shopping...again.

As I exited the store about one half hour later, he ran over to me and said, "M'am, I've been looking for you! I just wanted you to know that what you said may have changed my life. I was ready to give up and thought God couldn't use me in Christian work because I was a failure. But, if I just need to be available and He will do the rest, that's cool. I can do that!" He grabbed me and hugged me and thanked me for taking the time to talk to him. My heart was soaring as I drove home from the grocery store. Without the lonely times in my life, I don't think I would have been as sensitive to the leading of the Holy Spirit on that day.

Another time, I noticed a young mother in a restaurant who was weeping. She had three small children and looked so forlorn and lonely. I couldn't stand it. My heart was yearning to do something. As I watched, she got up and went to the restroom, leaving her small children in the hands of the oldest, who was about six years old. I asked my sweet husband to please go and take care of the children and I went looking for this dear mother. In the restroom, I found her weeping on the floor. Oh how she needed to know God loved her! She had recently moved into the area and was having such a difficult time with life. She had recently lost her husband and felt so alone. I told her that I was a grandmother of five and my husband was out telling stories to her children so she didn't need to worry. Then I shared God's love with her and prayed for God to meet her needs, right there in the restroom. How thankful I was that God had opened my eyes to notice His child who was hurting. Through this contact, she got into a good church, had renewed hope, and we developed a sweet friendship.

There were other things that God put on my heart during this time. He led me to reach out on holidays to those with no families because I now knew what it felt like to be alone on those days. And best of all, God showed me that true joy and contentment were found in loving and serving Him. Sometimes He blesses us with family and friends close by, and sometimes that isn't His plan for us. Either way, I discovered that I could have real peace and joy in being His child, and I could rejoice that He was maturing me and using me for His glory.

Truthfully, I'm so thankful for those lonely times. I never want to go back to my old perspective. It's so easy to draw inward when we're lonely. We quickly become self-centered and lose sight of what God's Word says in 2 Thessalonians 1:11-12:

To this end also we pray for you always that our God may count you worthy of your calling, and fulfill every desire for goodness and the work of faith with power; in order that the name of our Lord Jesus may be glorified in you, and you in Him, according to the grace of our God and the Lord Jesus Christ.

And again we are reminded what our purpose is.

For I live in eager expectation and hope that I will never do anything that causes me shame, but that I will always be bold for Christ,...and that my life will always honor Christ, whether I live or die. For to me, living is for Christ...

(Philippians 1:20,21 NLT)

If we believe God's Word, then we will know that our purpose in life, even in lonely times, is to bring honor to Christ. And, we might find that we are incredibly blessed by what God wants to do in us, through us, and for us as He expands our vision.

NANA'S STORY

It was Christmas time and our children and all of our grandchildren had come to celebrate at Nana and Papa's house. What fun we were having, just being together and sharing all the joys of the season. The grandkids were very young and usually liked to stay close to the adults. They'd bring their toys into the family room or kitchen and play near us, where they could hear our voices and feel secure. Little Jack especially loved being close by.

Anticipating the arrival of the family, I had decorated every inch of the house. But the main attraction was the full-size manger in the living room. Years ago, my husband built me a rough hewn manger which was just big enough for a life-sized baby. Each year I put fresh hay in it, wrap a porcelain baby doll in swaddling clothes and put it in the manger. There would be sheep lying around it and lighted trees behind it. Then the entire manger is wrapped in a huge gold bow with a gift tag on it. The tag simply reads, "For You." Nearby is a framed print of John 3:16. Anyone entering my home sees what we are celebrating and it has opened many conversations with people who come to our front door.

Now back to Jack. My daughter and I noticed that he wasn't in the small group playing near us in the kitchen so I went in search of him. I found him laying as close as possible to the manger, playing with his little army men. I asked him if he'd like to come out to the kitchen to be near us. His reply has stayed with me, "No thanks, Nana! I just want to stay close to Jesus!" You see, Jack didn't even notice that he was alone because he was conscious of staying close to Jesus, even though it was only a doll which represented Jesus.

Have you lost your awareness of Jesus' presence? Maybe your loneliness is God's way of bringing you closer to Himself. *"Do not fear, for I am with you."* (Isaiah 41:10a)

STAYING CLOSE TO JESUS

Staying close to Jesus
Feeling His presence, hearing His voice,
Making a good choice.

Staying close to Jesus
Knowing His love, trusting His plan,
Holding on to His hand.

Staying close to Jesus
Not looking to others, not going astray
Just trusting His way!

Carol Hopson

CHAPTER 4

WHEN GOD SEEMS GONE

Have you ever wondered where God is? You find yourself going through pain, disappointment, or defeat and you don't know how you will handle it. You try to pray and read the Bible but nothing seems to work; things don't change and life gets more difficult. Where is God when you're feeling like this? Why doesn't He make things right? I remember a very dark time in my life. My husband was suddenly without work, I was very sick, we were away from family and life-long friends, and it felt like God had abandoned us. No matter how hard I tried to trust, the nights were most difficult, and I'd wake up feeling alone and out of touch with my Savior.

Before I go on, I think it's time for my favorite eagle story. I've shared it with thousands of women and yet it excites me every time I tell it. It begins with how the eagles mate. The female eagle watches for a male that is interested in her and when she's ready to be courted, she flies down and picks up a twig or branch and brings it up high with her. She then drops the twig and watches to see if the male catches it before it hits the ground. If he catches it and returns it to her, she will find another larger or smaller stick to drop next time. She will continue to do this with various size branches and from various heights. If the male ever lets the branch hit the ground, she flies away and the courtship is over. She may do this over and over until she is satisfied that he will never allow the branch to hit the ground. For the final test, she will pick up a small log, almost as big as she is and fly swiftly in a figure eight pattern. She will stay very close to the ground and then suddenly drop the log and again test the male's athletic ability. If he succeeds, they will lock their talons and do a mating dance in flight and then they will mate for life.

In another chapter you'll learn how a baby eaglet leaves its nest, but now it's time to tell you that at a certain point of maturity, the mother eagle will shove her little eagle out of the nest and he will be frightened to death. He's never flown before and doesn't know what to expect, so it is a very scary time for him. He tries and tries to flap his wings fast enough to stay afloat but He is surely going to die when he hits the ground. But he doesn't know the plan. You see, just before he hits the ground, the father eagle swoops down under him and catches him on his wings and brings him back to the nest for his next flying lesson. Now you see why the female was so adamant about him catching the branch every single time.

I know it seems like God isn't involved with your life at times....but He is. And, He's always there to support you even when it doesn't feel like it. But He knows what's best for us and how much we need to learn in our circumstances. You see, I had counseled so many women in the past 30 years...women who had gone through such terrible tragedies. Some lost children to death or sinful choices, some lost husbands through abandonment or affairs, some had suffered through abortions and others had been abused beyond belief. Though I always had listening ears and a heart to help them, I never could identify with their hopelessness. I truly believe that God allowed me to go through those very dark days so that I could feel a little of what they felt and could therefore be more understanding in my counseling. From that point on, God gave me a different perspective on people who had no hope and He has enabled me, by His grace, to bring them hope and encouragement through a deeper understanding of His Word, His purpose and His sovereignty.

God reminds us how He took care of His people when they were fleeing from the Egyptians and they thought they would surely die.

You yourselves have seen what I did to the Egyptians, and how I bore you on eagles' wings and brought you to Myself.

(Exodus 19:4)

In praise to God, let me tell you how God swooped under us and saved us, just when we thought we were about to crash. We had been waiting eleven long months for direction, for a job, for what God wanted us to do. Then, just before we lost all hope, God did the following in a period of forty-eight hours:

- He gave us the exact ministry that we had desired and prayed for

- He sold our house to the first people that walked in

- He found a home for us to buy that was exactly what we needed

- He moved us to within two hours of our children and grandchildren

- He provided for our financial needs in miraculous ways

- He gave us willing, eager hearts to serve Him in our new ministry near San Diego, California

What a beautiful picture of our Heavenly Father's love and care for us. He certainly gave us a very important "flying lesson," and He taught us a great deal about resting in His loving arms when we couldn't understand what He was doing.

NANA'S STORY

We were vacationing with our children and grandchildren at a lovely resort. My husband was playing with the kids in the pool while I was playing in the sand with Lucy. Eventually, little 18-month old Lucy got tired and it was time for a nap but we weren't anywhere near a bed or room for her to sleep in. She had been trying to keep up with the bigger kids all morning and was now at the end of her energy. The problem was that she didn't know she was at the end and, like any toddler, she wanted to keep going as long as she possibly could. I tried to get her to lay down beside me on a chaise lounge and rest but that wasn't very appealing to an active toddler. Finally, when she couldn't keep the tears of fatigue away, I convinced her to lay in my lap on the lounge and just rest for a minute while I sang to her. She climbed up in her little yellow swimsuit and layed her precious body on mine. As I stroked her little blond curls and began to sing to her, she began to relax. Now Lucy was never the type to stay still for long, so any moments of cuddling were precious to me. I knew she'd probably jump up at the end of the song but for some reason she didn't move. I asked my daughter if she was asleep but she said she wasn't. I began another song and another and I could feel Lucy's body totally let go and melt into mine as she gave up and truly rested in my arms.

My active granddaughter stayed in my arms for 45 minutes without stirring, yet without sleeping. I was in heaven! How I loved holding her chubby little body, smelling her hair, and feeling her breathing so close to my heart. It was at this time that God taught me a wonderful truth. I realized that as Lucy gave in to the rest she so desperately needed, my joy was increased immeasurably because I was the one who could give her that rest. I was the one that she trusted enough to give herself over to, and the joy of those moments was so precious to me. I then realized that this must be how my Savior feels. He's waiting for me to let go, give up my struggles, and truly rest in His loving care. But what's more important than that to me is that my resting in Him must bring Him great joy....because He loves me so much! It hurts me to realize that I'm robbing Him of something precious to Him when I don't trust Him enough to rest in His plan and His care for me.

In repentance and rest you shall be saved, in quietness and trust is your strength...

(Isaiah 30:15a)

THE JOY OF RESTING

She ran around from dawn to dusk
Just like a little pup.
She swam and ran and climbed and tried
To keep her spirits up.

Though only two, she wanted so
To stay up all day long
And do the things that others did
Was that so very wrong?

But as I took her in my arms
I saw her weariness.
I held her close and stroked her hair
With joy, I must confess.

As she began to give in to
Her Nana's warm embrace
I saw such sweet contentment on
That precious little face.

I run around from dawn ' til dusk
Just like a little pup
And try to keep my spirits high
And all my work keep up.

And sometimes God just needs to say
"Come, child, it's time to rest!"
And yet I fight it, doing things
I feel are still the best.

But lovingly, He draws me in
To fellowship with Him
And helps me find a place of rest
As other things grow dim.

I'm learning now to seek this place
Of comfort so divine.
And as I rest I see the joy it brings
His heart and mine.

Carol Hopson

CHAPTER 5

LIVING BY FAITH

The early development of the eaglet is very important to the parents and to its future survival. For this reason, both parents spend most of the first two weeks with the eaglets. The female does her shading and brooding of her chicks, while the male provides nearly all the food. If the female feels the need to leave the nest for a short time, the male replaces her. Remember, this is when the babies are the most vulnerable to the serpent's attacks. During the first few weeks, the mother eagle will take the food the father has brought back and will tear it into small pieces and feed it to her babies. But, after a few weeks, things begin to change and she stops tearing the food up for them. At five weeks, they can do it on their own, but she must stop doing it for them or they will never learn to tear it up for themselves. About two weeks before the eaglets leave the nest, there is a marked drop in the amount of food brought back to the nest for them. They probably don't understand what is happening, or why, but if they were always "provided for" they would never desire to leave the nest and become healthy, mature eagles.

As the young eagles learn to venture out and fly, their hunting skills will take some time to develop, and they will often come back to their nest to beg their parents for "easy" food. But the wise parents refuse to feed their young and will actually chase them away from the nest, knowing that they need to develop these skills as quickly as possible. You see, they seem to know that the easiest way is not usually the best way! It doesn't bring maturity, strength, or proper growth.

I can't tell you how many times God has taken me away from the "easy" path and has lovingly guided me toward the "strengthening" or "growing" path. Let me give you an example of this. When God put it on our hearts to start a Christian school in a new place, with no board, no money, no buildings, and no teachers, we thought we'd see Him provide miraculously for our needs, especially since we had stepped out in faith and left our secure position to do this. Sometimes, He did do miracles on our behalf. And yet, there were many times that we felt like He was "shooing us away" from the easy path, and letting us learn to trust in the midst of nearly impossible circumstances.

For months we had been faithfully praying for a building to house our new school, but God didn't provide one until five days before our school was scheduled to open! Then we couldn't move in for two more days, giving us three days to move walls, clean out years of filth, put down carpets, add lighting, chalkboards, heaters, desks and all the other things a school of K-8 would need. God could have given us weeks or even months to get ready for the opening of school...but He chose not to...because we needed to learn to trust Him completely for our needs. We also needed to learn that God would enable us to do the "impossible" as we trusted His timing and His plan.

We prayed for funds to take us through the first few months of operation, but God decided that we needed to live totally by faith, day by day, week by week, and so there was never a penny more than we needed. Often, payday would come and we wouldn't have the needed money to pay our staff, but God would then provide at the ninth hour, after our faith had again been tested and strengthened. After two years in our small building, we had outgrown it as a school. We then sought to move or purchase land and build a new site for our growing Christian school. But, God had us try seventeen different times to relocate or build, and each time we were shut down by the city council, the planning commission, or by other problems. This continued over a period of fourteen years...growing years...maturing years...God's years!

After fourteen years, God miraculously provided a whole new school for us...free of charge. It was better than anything we ever dreamed of. But, during the long waiting season, it often seemed like we were never going to be able to move. However, God wanted others to see our faithfulness despite things not going our way. We heard from several members of the community that they were watching to see how those "Christians" handled disappointments and the unfair treatment by the city planners and the press. It was a small community where everyone knew what was going on, and they wanted to know if what we taught in the school was real in our lives.

I could relate so many stories of what God took my husband and me though during those years, but the most important thing to tell you is that He was always faithful! He knew what was best for us and He knew how we needed to grow in order to be able to handle what He had for us in the future. He was truly preparing us to "walk in His steps" each moment and not be discouraged by the circumstances or the impossibilities. Little did we know how much we would need these "lessons" in the future, but He knew! In the books, *"But God, This Wasn't My Plan!"* and *"But God, I'm Tired of Waiting!"* I continue this story and tell what God was preparing us for.

I used to wonder why Paul had to endure so much during his years of ministry. Why did God allow things to be so difficult when he was choosing to serve the Lord so faithfully? But, as I've studied the books of the New Testament that Paul has penned, I've realized that the disappointments, the imprisonments, the beatings, the betrayals by friends and the changed plans are what make his testimony and his faithfulness to the Lord so real and powerful in my life. I've read his books over and over and memorized large portions of them and they have always encouraged, challenged, and uplifted me. When Paul says, *"For me to live is Christ...,"* I know he means it and I can see how he lived that out in various situations.

When he says:

Your attitude should be the same that Christ Jesus had. Though he was God, he did not demand and cling to his rights as God. He made himself nothing, he took the humble position of a slave, and he appeared in human form. And in human form he obediently humbled himself even further by dying a criminal's death on a cross.

(Philippians 2:5-8 NLT)

44

I realize that God can enable me to have this attitude also as I empty self and humbly obey...especially when it makes no sense to me!

When I read Paul's words in 2 Corinthians 12:9a:

> *My gracious favor is all you need. My power works best in your weakness...*

I'm extremely encouraged because I know Paul learned this through the difficulties he faced, not through a life of comfort and ease. Therefore, I can relate to him and can trust my Father just as he did and find peace.

The next time you feel like God is robbing you of something you need, want, or deserve, remember that He is allowing this for your maturity, just as a father loves his child and wants the best for him.

NANA'S STORY

When my grandchildren come for a visit, my life changes. I change my schedule, cancel unnecessary appointments, shop for foods I never have in the house, search garage sales for new toys to please them, and so on. I purchase little gifts for each one and make sure there are goodies in the pantry. I pray for sunshine so we can walk to the park, go to the beach, or play in the back yard. When they're here, I color, play with dolls, horses, Legos, and trucks, push them on swings, and wake up extra early to a grandchild's desire to snuggle in Nana and Papa's bed. It sounds like I would do most anything for these precious grandchildren, doesn't it? Yet, there are times when Nana has to say, "No, you can't have any more sweets today, because you might get sick." Or, "I know you'd rather stay up late with us, but you need your rest so you'll be able to play tomorrow and not get too tired."

Children often don't understand this and think it is mean. They especially try to maneuver and charm their grandparents into bending the rules. Of course, Nana and Papa do get to bend some of the rules at times, (like having sugar-coated cereals in all shapes and colors) but never to the detriment of the child. Because we love them, we must keep their best interest foremost when they are with us. That is the loving thing to do. Sometimes, it's very difficult to not give in to them because they associate "their desires" with love, but we know that is only immature thinking. And so, out of our love, we do what is best, not what makes them feel good at the time.

I often think it must be difficult for our Heavenly Father to watch us struggle when we don't understand what He's doing in our lives. So, how do we learn to accept this kind of love?

Let the words of Christ, in all their richness, lie in your hearts and make you wise. Use his words to teach and counsel each other. Sing psalms and hymns and spiritual songs to God with thankful hearts. And whatever you do or say, let it be as a representative of the Lord Jesus, all the while giving thanks through him to God the Father.

(Colossians 3:16-18 NLT)

TO HAVE MY WAY

Sometimes I think it would be great
To always get my way.
To have things go as I had planned
And never feel dismay.

But that is foolishness to God
Who knows what's best for me,
For he knows what is needed and
He does it lovingly.

It doesn't feel like love when He
Allows such hurtful things,
But I must know Him well enough
To not keep pulling strings.

And so as I grow more in love
My own desires grow dim.
I learn to trust my Father's plan
And leave all things to Him.

Carol Hopson

CHA6TER

PREPARING FOR LIFE

Baby eaglets have a great life. They live in a soft, furry down that their mother has plucked from her own breast and placed in their nest. Their father brings them toys and food and meets their every need. Life is good, life is fun, life has no worries. But then one day, life changes. Without warning, the mother eagle begins to remove all of the soft lining of their home, and then even takes away the soft leaves and small branches that have brought them security and comfort. There's nothing left but large, scratchy branches which the young eagles have to clamp on to with their little talons. It's not fun! It's scary... and then the mother leaves them for a while and they have to manage by themselves. What has happened? Why is their mother so cruel?

Day after day they have to struggle like this, holding on to those branches for all they are worth so they don't fall through the cracks. Why is life suddenly so cruel and what has happened to their mother's love? She certainly couldn't love them any more if she's making them go through such a hard time every day. But the young eagles only see their discomfort and not the purpose of their trial.

You see, their mother knows what they need to learn, that developing strong talons is essential to survival. They will use their talons to procure fish or a rabbit or other food for the rest of their lives. However, in the early stages of gaining strength, the young eagles are unaware that this "cruel" treatment is preparing them for success in life. Each day of balancing and grasping those branches is strengthening their young talons.

Like those eagles, we too lose sight of the fact that the trials which we face are for our success and not to defeat us.

God tells us so clearly,

> *Consider it all joy, my brethren, when you encounter various trials, knowing that the testing of your faith produces endurance. And let endurance have its perfect result, that you may be perfect and complete, lacking in nothing.*
>
> (James 1:2-4)

My life would be so much easier if I accepted this more readily, wouldn't yours? Why do we question what God is doing every time we face a test or trial?

The reason I do it is because my mind has focused on what I want instead of what God wants. I quickly forget that I am created by God, loved by God, forgiven by God and therefore God desires the very best for me. He wants me to be strong and ready to handle whatever life brings...and so each trial or difficult situation is strengthening my "talons" for future success. He does it because he loves me so much! Let me share the same verse again in another version.

Dear brothers and sisters, whenever trouble comes your way, let it be an opportunity for joy. For when your faith is tested, your endurance has a chance to grow. So let it grow, for when your endurance is fully developed, you will be strong in character and ready for anything.

(James 1:2-4 NLT)

Let me share a time when God was definitely strengthening my "talons" in preparation for the future. All the soft downy fur of my security had suddenly been ripped out and I found myself asking what God was doing. I had been told that four mammograms and two ultrasounds revealed a mass which had the doctors very concerned. As I left the doctor's office, I had a choice to make. So, after two consultations, I decided to go ahead with the surgery they were suggesting. During the three months of appointments leading up to this, the Lord was strengthening my talons. I had to learn to release my fears and trust Him a little more each day. I was speaking to many groups during those months. Often, they asked me to speak on topics such as *"Peace in the Midst"* or *"Living by Faith"* or *"Waiting with Purpose and Power."* These were not easy days, in fact they were uncomfortable at times because I had to go through 6 different appointments in the span of three months. Then I'd have to wait for the results and schedule a follow-up appointment. This happened over and over. Yet, I knew that God was strengthening me for whatever would lie ahead. When the day of the scheduled surgery came, God had so prepared me that my heart was incredibly peaceful. This was definitely a miracle, and not anything I could conjure up.

I spent about one and a half hours with the nurse who prepped me for surgery. She had dealt with breast cancer patients all day, every day, for over ten years. She naturally assumed that I was very nervous. She asked me several times if I was okay and I told her each time that I was at peace with whatever God chose for me. I explained that I had given my life to the Lord because of my love for Him, and it was up to Him to choose the path my life would take. I told her that my greatest joy was in loving and serving Him. She looked at me like I was from a different planet and kept pursuing it with me. All the while, she was looking at the mammograms, arranging things, and getting me ready.

As things turned out, the mass was not cancer, and not anything life-threatening. The surgeon had decided, just before cutting, to take a fifth mammogram and it was after studying that fifth one that she and another doctor discovered that the "mass" was only a strange alignment of blood vessels and I needed no surgery or further treatment. After the surgeon left, the nurse came up to my bed and said, "Could you please tell me how to find the peace that you have." What a privilege to share God's love and peace with her before going out to tell my husband the great news.

I realized then, that God had taken me through this long journey so that He could do His work in me. Then when His timing was right, He used my circumstance and the peace that only He can give, to bring a young nurse the message of His love and renewed hope. Always remember that we seldom see the big picture when God is removing some of our comforts, but it's always for our good. (Romans 8:28)

Is God strengthening your talons right now? Why not change your perspective and thank Him for loving you enough to care about your maturity and growth. Then ask Him to use you for His glory in whatever circumstance He has allowed. You'll never regret that decision!

NANA'S STORY

I was going to visit my daughter and her three children at a park. I was on my way to a speaking engagement that was halfway between her house and mine, and so we arranged to meet. I was dressed for a fancy luncheon, but that didn't matter as I love any opportunity to see my daughter and grandchildren. As we arrived at the park, the boys took off to kick some balls around, and Lucy Marie headed for the toddler play area. My daughter and I settled on a bench where we could watch all of them but especially close to the toddler play area. I was cheering Lucy on as she played on the various structures when she called out to me, "C'mon Nana!" "I see you Lucy!" I responded and cheered her on with her endeavors. That didn't seem to satisfy her, as she called again and motioned with her chubby little hand for me to come over by her. So, being an obedient Nana, I got up and went over and stood by the play structure. Yes, I had my dress, nylons, and heels on but Lucy was calling and so I went. I thought surely this would satisfy her and tried to get her to go down the slide but she stood above me and called, "C'mon Nana!" And again, that chubby little hand motioned for me to join her. How foolish, I can't climb up there with my heels and dress on....but I did! With all the mothers watching, and my daughter laughing out loud, I climbed up the little ladder and stood on top like a giant. Surely this was enough to satisfy Lucy! I told her I'd clap as she slid down the tube slide, but as she sat down at the entrance and turned to look at me, I knew what was coming. "C'mon Nana!" and that was all it took. In my good dress, nylons, jewelry, and heels, I straddled my granddaughter and headed down the covered slide with her...but only Lucy came out the other end. Nana got stuck! I heard laughter outside and saw Lucy's little face peering in at the bottom questioning, "Nana, where are you?" I was stuck! Those slides are not made for adult size hips! But, after shifting around I finally got to the bottom...and even did it again!

Why would I do such a thing? Why would I make such a fool of myself...in public? Because I love Lucy so much and I didn't want to disappoint her. I love seeing the smile it brings to her face when I come and do what she asks of me. Why, then, do I not easily follow my Lord in whatever He asks of me...simply for the joy it brings to Him?

LUCY MARIE

She called my name, I turned my head
To see her beckoning
For me to come and play with her
And push her on the swing.

Not yet two years, her sparkling eyes
And chubby little hand
Took me down slides I couldn't fit,
I was at her command.

You see, this grandchild, yet so small
Has taken o'er my heart.
And when she calls "C'mon, Nana!"
I gladly do my part.

Now why is it so difficult
To listen to my Lord,
And hear Him say, "C'mon, dear one,
I want to show you more."

Why do I hesitate to trust
The One who died for me?
Why don't I jump when He says "Come"
And follow willingly.

It's not an easy thing to tell,
I've known it from the start.
When I don't obey Him it's because
He doesn't have my heart!

Carol Hopson

CHAPTER 7

RISING ABOVE THE STORMS

Have you ever watched an eagle in flight? It's incredible and majestic, but what's even more amazing is how an eagle handles a storm. The eagle is very different from all other creatures, in that it doesn't seek cover or get nervous and jittery as a storm approaches. You see, an eagle is prepared for whatever the storm brings because he has spent years studying storms and weather currents and knows what to look for, what to expect, and how to handle it. Before mating, an eagle spends about 3 years soaring high above the earth in various weather patterns because he is learning how to handle everything life will bring in the future. He knows that safety is found high above the storm so he learns how to use the currents that each storm brings, to raise him up above the dangerous winds. It seems that he practices this until it becomes second nature.

The eagle sits calmly as the storm approaches, and knows what to do because of his preparation. When he is ready, he locks his wings into an ascending position and "mounts up" into the storm and lets the currents lift him up to where the sun is shining. The storm is still raging, but he has put it beneath him, where it doesn't affect him, and he soars in the beauty of the sunshine. It's so interesting to me that he "locks his wings" into an ascending position. To ascend means to move upward or rise gradually, and so, as the eagle locks his wings, he makes up his mind to purposefully move upward. Isn't this what God has called us to do?

> *If you have been raised up with Christ, keep seeking the things above, where Christ is seated at the right hand of God. Set your mind on the things above, not on the things that are on earth.*
>
> (Colossians 3:1,2)

He desires that we continually look upward at the truth and not downward as the storms rage, because that is where victory is found. I love what Corrie Ten Boom used to say while she was imprisoned in Auschwitz. *"Look within and be depressed, look around and be distressed, look to Jesus and be at rest."*

The picture of the eagle rising above the storm is also a definite reminder of Isaiah 40:31:

> *They that wait on the Lord shall renew their strength; they shall mount up with wings as eagles...*

There have certainly been many times in my life that I would have loved to "mount up" above the storm and see the sun, but I didn't take advantage of the "currents" God had provided for me through His precious Word. As I've learned this truth, God has helped me see things with a different perspective and He has enabled me to rise above many storms that were raging around me.

Let me give you an example of this. When faced with a very unjust and cruel situation, my first impulse was to be angry and harbor bitterness. But knowing that this wasn't God's way (Hebrews 12:15), I began calling to mind the "currents" I had studied from God's Word. I recalled Psalm 37:8 which warns:

> *Cease from anger, and forsake wrath; do not fret, it leads only to evildoing.*

Then I remembered how the righteous are supposed to react:

> *The mouth of the righteous utters wisdom, and his tongue speaks justice. The law of His God is in his heart; his steps do not slip.*
>
> (Psalm 37:30,31)

You see, these were the currents I needed to help me let go of the anger and rise above it, and then keep my words and thoughts pure in obedience to the Lord.

I also remembered Psalm 55:22 which promises:

> *Cast your burden on the Lord and He will sustain you; He will never allow the righteous to be shaken.*

This gave me comfort and assurance whenever I needed it. But, the choice was mine, moment by moment. I could choose to be pulled under by the storm or I could choose, out of love for my Lord, to rise above it. I also knew that if I chose to "mount up," God was ready to help me *"will and do His good pleasure."* (Philippians 2:14)

Sometimes, it's very difficult to resist the pull of the storm and we let our minds to be pulled down with doubts or fears. But, we need to trust our Heavenly Father, and what He is doing for our good. Arthur Tappan Pierson wrote the following:

> *He will sit as a refiner and purifier of silver.*
>
> (Malachi 3:3)

> *"Our Father, who seeks to perfect His saints in holiness, knows the value of the refiner's fire. It is with the most precious metals that a metallurgist will take the greatest care. He subjects the metal to a hot fire, for only the refiner's fire will melt the metal, release the dross, and allow the remaining, pure metal to take a new and perfect shape in the mold.*
> *"A good refiner never leaves the crucible but, as the above verse indicates, "will sit" down by it so the fire will not become even one degree too hot and possibly harm the metal. And as soon as he skims the last bit of dross from the surface and sees his face reflected in the pure metal, he extinguishes the fire."*

Oh, if only I would quickly see the storm as the fiery process God is using to make me look like Him!

Recently, someone asked me what was the greatest lesson I'd learned in the past years of brokenness and changed plans. My quick response was...to let go of my plans and accept God's plan for me with joy. This is where true peace and fulfillment are found. There is nothing to compare with knowing that you are God's child and you are fulfilling what He created you to do. Paul knew this truth and lived by it.

All the things I once thought were so important are gone from my life. Compared to the high privilege of knowing Christ Jesus as my Master, firsthand, everything I once thought I had going for me is insignificant...dog dung. I've dumped it in the trash so that I could embrace Christ and be embraced by Him.

(Philippians 3:7,8)

Once we realize that our plans, our earthly treasures, our desires to have our own way...are all "dog dung" or "garbage" in God's sight, we can learn to "mount up with wings as eagles" and soar. My husband and I have been asked to give up honor and accept humility, give up dreams and accept growth, give up security and accept living by faith. But I wouldn't give up a moment of it. How thankful I am that God continually reminds me that "His ways are not my ways" and I've chosen His way...for life!

Nana's Story

Jack and Elliot loved the new set of army men I bought for them. Each time they visit, I like to have a new surprise toy that they haven't seen before and this time it was an army camp, equipped with helicopters, tanks, men, and lots of other things they loved. The problem was that I only purchased one set and both boys wanted to play with it all the time. Who would get the helicopter and who could have the tank, and for how long? Oh my, it was new and exciting to them and therefore it was not only a cause for joy, but also for sibling rivalry. Well, this Nana learned her lesson and the next time they visited, I had two sets of army men awaiting them. I could hardly wait to see their eyes when they saw that they could each have a set all the time. But something had happened! It wasn't that much fun to play with them now that they each had one, and they had moved on to other things so the army camp wasn't that popular anymore. I realize that this is fairly normal for kids: they absolutely have to have something one time, and then when they get it and play with it a little bit, it gets old and loses its attraction.

When faced with those daily storms, I realized that what I so desperately wanted one day, would lose its attraction the next day because a new situation or problem had come on the scene. As I gave in to the wrong thoughts and attitudes, which felt so good for the moment, my heart was plunged into negativity and discouragement. I realized that I needed to let the Lord be the stability of my times and not be controlled by my emotions. I had to repent of being fickle in my desires, at times, just like my precious grandchildren, and then I needed to thank Him that His presence and power in my life are always totally sufficient. (2 Corinthians 12:9) Finally, I needed to thank Him that He was refining me so that He could see Himself in me.

ON EAGLE'S WINGS

The eagle soars above the storm
Without fear or unrest.
He has a plan, he lifts his wings
And does what he knows best.

He seems to know a secret that
Helps him to stay up high.
He's learned from past experience
Just where he needs to fly.

The Eagle takes the currents that
Could easily distress,
And lets it lift his wings to where
He finds such peace and rest.

Now I would like to soar above
The storms that come my way
And I would like to rise above
And never feel dismay.

I think I need to take God's Word
As storm clouds gather 'round
And let its truths give my heart wings
So fear cannot be found.

And as I trust the truths I read
And to them always cling
I know my God will help me rise
And soar on eagle's wings.

Carol Hopson

CHAPTER 8

LEARNING TO FLY

I love reading about how the mother and father eagles take care of their little family. They build a huge nest, made up of large branches, smaller twigs and leaves, and soft downy feathers from the mother's breast. After the eaglets are hatched, the father eagle goes in search of food, and eventually he hunts for toys and returns with a ball, a shoe, a tin can or something else he found in someone's backyard. These will keep the babies happy and entertained for awhile. They are safe and secure in their nest and everything they need is brought to them.

But as they begin to mature, life changes for them. You've already read how their mother strips away their toys and all of the soft lining of their home. But she eventually goes further than that. After she sees that their little talons are getting stronger and stronger, she takes them to another stage of development. One day, she begins moving them toward the edge of their safe nest. This nest is usually eight to twelve feet across and so the young birds haven't had to venture this close to the edge before. She pushes and prods them up toward the rim of the nest until they are just balancing on the edge. I'm sure they're wondering what's happened to their loving mother. How could she be so mean? The Scriptures even mention the female eagle that *"stirs up her nest."* (Deuteronomy 32:11)

Just when they start getting used to balancing on the edge, she takes her wing and flicks one of them out of the nest. What a shock! How could this be happening? They were in such a nice, safe environment and now they've been flung out into the cruel world. The eaglet probably assumes death is near as he tries and tries to flap his wings but keeps falling downward.

Wow, I've felt just like that little eagle! I've felt safe and secure in my home and my circumstances and life were going along so well. Then, without warning, I was flung out into a desperate situation and felt that I was truly going to crash, die, or even worse...not die. How could a loving Father allow this to happen to His child? How could He allow such cruelty, such unexpected changes, such insecurity? The simple answer is...because He loves me. It's just that I don't always understand His love, just as a small child can't understand the discipline or discipleship of his parent because he doesn't have the maturity. He just has to trust his parent's love.

Our Heavenly Father says:

I know the plans I have for you, declares the Lord,

plans for welfare and not for calamity, to give you
a future and a hope.

(Jeremiah 29:11)

I had to love God enough to trust Him and choose to believe that He was giving me a future and a hope when I was told that the baby I was carrying would most likely die or be born with severe problems. I had hemorraged at three and a half months, on an airplane, and was encouraged to abort the baby if I didn't miscarry in the near future. We had prayed for this child and already loved this child so much. We would never consider abortion and so we had to take just one day at a time and trust that God knew what was best for us. We also had to continually remember how much He loved us and this special child I was carrying. To the doctor's amazement, our perfect, beautiful daughter was born without any of the predicted problems. What if we would have believed the advice we received and didn't trust God enough to know what was best for us? This was such a life-altering lesson for me. I realized that I could have wasted six precious months worrying, fretting, and being angry with God over something that was never going to happen. I'm sure there have been many times in my life when I did jump to wrong conclusions and didn't believe what God's Word so clearly teaches. It's so important to do what David did.

I have set the Lord continually before me; because
He is at my right hand, I will not be shaken.
Therefore my heart is glad and my glory rejoices;
my flesh also shall dwell securely.

(Psalm 16:8,9)

Now let's get back to that little flailing eaglet. He still thinks he's going to crash and life is over. But, just before he hits the ground, the father eagle, swoops under him and catches him on his back and returns him to his nest for another flying lesson. Isn't that a beautiful picture of God's loving care for us? We can't learn obedience in our comfortable surroundings, and we can't grow properly if we never learn to crawl, walk, and run. And so, God, in His love, gives us "flying lessons." God knows what's ahead and He knows how He wants to use us and so we need to trust Him with the lessons He has planned for us.

Always remember that God has promised:

I am the Lord your God, who upholds your right hand, who says to you, 'Do not fear, I will help you.'

(Isaiah 41:12)

Nana's Story

Since Lucy is my youngest grandchild, I seem to have more recent stories about her, so I'll share one more at this point. I think this is one of the greatest lessons I've learned through my precious grandchildren. Ten-month-old Lucy was playing in the family room which adjoined our kitchen. I was getting dinner ready and the family was outside enjoying the back yard. After checking to see where Lucy was, I opened my lower oven door and pulled out the casserole. I took it to the counter and then returned to close the oven door. But to my horror, little Lucy had somehow crawled all that way in seconds and was now reaching for the 400 degree oven door. She was used to playing with the dishwasher door which was at the same level, and she didn't know the difference. In my panic, all I could think of to do was to reach out and fling her away from the hot oven door, just as she was reaching for it. She fell back on her little bottom and looked up at me with quivering lips and tear-filled eyes. It was as if she was saying to me, "Nana, I thought you loved me! How could you be so mean to me! You're the one who sings to me, cuddles me, and lights up when I enter the room. Why would you knock me down like that?" Now, did I do this because I didn't care or didn't love her? Did I do it to punish her? Of course not! I did it solely out of my deep love for her, to protect her, but she couldn't understand that yet.

My heart was shaken by the near tragedy and by Lucy's look of disbelief. All I could do was to rush to her, pick her up, and hold her tight. I took her to the chair and began to sing to her and rock her in my arms. You see, there was no way I could explain to a ten-month-old why I had to react the way I did. She was too young and her understanding was too limited. All I could do was to remind her of my love and hold her until she remembered and rested in my arms. Gradually, Lucy relaxed, her tears ceased and she was once again my trusting little grandchild.

As I sat rocking her for a long time, God revealed to me a truth that has carried me through many struggles. Sometimes, I feel so knocked down by the circumstances He allows and I wonder what He is doing. But then I realize that my understanding is so limited and I can't know the mind of God, but I can and do know how much He loves me. So, I just need to trust His love and leave the rest to Him.

Trust in the Lord with all your heart; do not depend on your own understanding. Seek His will in all you do and He will direct your paths.
(Proverbs 3:5,6 NLT)

I'm so thankful for this picture of God's loving care and protection. As I constantly remember His sacrificial love for me and all He's carried me through in the past, I cease to struggle with what He's doing in the present. I now know Him well enough to believe that He has only my good in His heart, and so I can rest and trust Him with whatever He allows. Thank You, God, for this beautiful picture of your love for me!

WHEN I DON'T UNDERSTAND

Dear God, Sometimes it's difficult
to see Your loving hand,
When people do such hurtful things
It's hard to understand.

It doesn't feel like love when You
allow such hurt and pain.
At times I've felt betrayed, alone
but Your love still remained.

I've learned through yet another child
just how You're watching me
And how the things that seem so hard
will truly set me free.

For as I learn to trust Your love
when I don't understand,
You'll hold me close, sing to my soul
and work out Your great plan.

CHAPTER 9

FACING THE PULL
OF THE WORLD

You're cheating on God. If all you want is your own way, flirting with the world every chance you get, you end up enemies of God and his way.

(James 4:4)

Why do we continue to flirt with the world? Why are we attracted to the pull of the world and why do we think there is more joy there? Let me explain. Recently, my heart has been heavy over a friend's decision to turn against God's ways and reject the truths of His Word. She had been "working for" the Lord for many years but then a "friend" came into her life and enticed her to see what the world had to offer. My friend took her eyes off of the truth, stopped reading God's Word and fellowshiping with believers, and Satan quickly lured her into a life of sin. I stayed in contact with her for many months, loving her and trying to call her back to the truth, but she got farther and farther into her sinful ways. She finally broke off all communication, but in our last talks I could see how empty and hopeless her life had become, and yet she chose to stay...hoping that the thrill would return.

Another woman I've counseled stepped out of God's will and went along with Satan's enticement for a time. She left her husband and children, thinking that the grass would be greener with a new man in her life. But, this situation ended differently. She tried to find peace and joy in the midst of her choices but she couldn't. Oh yes, there would be moments of happiness when she would enjoy the temporary excitement of sinful pleasures, but it never lasted and then guilt and sadness would overwhelm her. She was under conviction all the time, and couldn't ignore the pain any longer. She finally repented of her sinful choices, asked forgiveness of her family and went back home. God honored her obedience and healed her marriage and restored her joy. Yes, there are still consequences because of her choices, but she knows she is forgiven and her heart is at peace.

What made the difference in these two situations? I'll explain it with another eagle story. The eagle's eyes are truly amazing. You see, their eyes are made up of a series of tissues that are folded into pleats called pectins. There are tubes running thoughout these pleats which are filled with an electrolyte fluid which is a conductor of electricity and is affected by a magnetic field. Amazingly, these pectins align themselves with the North Pole in relation to the eagle's place of birth. By the time they are mature, the alignment is permanently set. Therefore, when the eagle is far from home, there is actually pain or discomfort in his eyes. The pain or pressure stops only when the eagle returns to his place of birth. This is why he can find his way home from thousands of miles away...God has given him a built-in compass.

God has done the same thing for His beloved children. He has given us the Holy Spirit, our "built-in" Compass, to convict and guide us through life. In the book of John we read,

> *But the Helper, the Holy Spirit, whom the Father will send in my name, He will teach you all things, and bring to your remembrance all that I said to you.*
> *And He, when He comes, will convict the world concerning sin, and righteousness and judgment.*
> (John 14:26 and 16:8)

I've certainly experienced this "pain or pressure" from the Holy Spirit when I've allowed bitterness to take root in my heart, or when I've knowingly said something hurtful. I've also felt it when I've been unwilling to do God's will because it was in conflict with what I wanted. It wasn't until I confessed my sin, and returned "home" to my Savior, that my peace was restored.

I love to read the Psalms because I often feel like David did, and I love His honesty.

He acknowledged,

> *When I kept it all inside, my bones turned to powder, my words became daylong groans. The pressure never let up; all the juices of my life dried up. Then I let it all out; I said, 'I'll make a clean breast of my failures to God.' Suddenly the pressure was gone, my guilt dissolved, my sin disappeared.*
> (Psalm 32:3-5 The Message)

75

The difference in the reaction of the two women I wrote about is this. The first woman was "working for God" and trying to be a Christian by doing good things. However, after getting to know her better, I realized that she had never committed her life to the Lord and had never received Him as her Lord and Savior. Therefore, she could continue in her life of sin and not feel the "pull" of conviction on her life. I saw hopelessness and defeat in her, but not conviction. I still pray that she will truly find peace by turning from her worldly life and by receiving God's free gift of forgiveness and salvation.

The second woman belonged to the Lord and He wouldn't let her go. The pull to return home was too great because of the Holy Spirit residing in her. I'm so thankful that God loves us enough to give us this spiritual "compass" to continually guide us through the difficult times and keep us from the attractions of the world. If you're feeling overwhelmed, enticed, convicted or miserable today, check your "compass" and start heading home.

NANA'S STORY

My husband decided to take little Monica and Becca for a walk while we were visiting them. He loved any chance to be with his granddaughters and cherished their hugs and kisses. He could always make any walk adventurous, and they knew it, so they eagerly joined him for this "safari" into the wild. As they headed out through fields and trees behind their home, my husband offered to carry little two-year-old Becca. He could see that this was quite an effort for her as there were rocks and logs to step over and he could see she was weary. But, being a normal two-year-old, she said she could do it by herself. However, as the hike grew longer, Becca finally looked up at her Papa and said, "Papa, I can't do it by'self. Pease carry me!"

Now what do you think her loving Papa said in reply? Do you think he said, "Becca, I'm too tired and don't feel like carrying you right now." Or do you suppose he shamed her for getting tired and admitting she needed his help? Of course not! My husband loves those grandchildren more than his own life and He will do anything to have them curl up in his arms so that he can have the chance to snuggle with them. So, he looked at Becca with heartfelt love and scooped her up into his arms and carried her the rest of the way, loving every minute of it. He was so glad that she wanted to be held that it was the first thing he told me when he got back.

Then I realized that this is the way my Heavenly Father feels about me, His beloved child. He loves me so much and wants to relieve the weight and stress of my journey...if I will only ask.

Cast your burden upon the Lord, and He will sustain you; He will never allow the righteous to be shaken.

(Psalm 55:22)

God, I can't do it by myself; will You please carry me today?

FATHER, WILL YOU CARRY ME?

Father, will you carry me?
I'm tired and can't go on.
I've tried to keep on going but
I've lost my joy and song.

You see, I tried to do it all
So You'd be proud of me.
But all I did was burn right out
As others 'round me see.

"Oh precious child, my heart is filled
With joy because you asked
For Me to carry you today
That is My rightful task."

"I've longed to hold you in my arms
And give you peace and rest
But first you had to see your need
And willingly confess."

So now I'm thrilled beyond compare
These times are far too few.
For now you've given up your pride
And let Me carry you.

Carol Hopson

CHAPTER 10

MY SOURCE OF STRENGTH

The soaring technique God has given the eagle is just amazing, and I think we can learn from it. When an eagle needs to gain height as he scans the ground for food, he doesn't waste his energy using powerful wing beats. Instead, he knows to find an air current rising from a patch of warm ground and then he circles in the rising air with out-spread wings. It's the rising air that carries him upward, not his efforts!

This soaring technique is very helpful during migration since he travels long distances at a time. When an eagle is going to have long periods in the air, he will seek out hotspots and updrafts to carry him so that he doesn't wear out on the jour-ney. He has also learned to avoid large, open stretches of water where there are no currents, because he knows he will get too tired to make the trip successfully.

Wow, these are such great lessons for me. How easily I forget that nothing of value is done in my strength! God is not impressed with me when I wear myself out trying to be all things to all people. Nor does He love me any more because I'm going day and night trying to "serve" Him. What he truly desires of me is that I learn how to "quit flapping my wings" and then use the updrafts of His Word to give me strength.

It's deeply engraved on my heart how God spoke to me about this. After a huge move to another state, I remember sitting in the family room wondering what God had for me. I had been so busy before this move and now had nothing to "do" for Jesus except be a support for my husband and keep a good home. I wasn't leading a Bible Study or speaking at retreats or working with my husband or taking care of my grandchildren or leading a choir and so on. As the tears began to gather in my eyes that rainy morning, I asked God, "What can I do for you when I have no place to serve you?" And, as soon as I said it, God's loving answer came to me. "My child, I don't want you to always "do" things for me, I want you to just "be" my child and love me. Paul realized the importance of this truth when he wrote:

That I may know Him, and the power of His resurrection and the fellowship of His sufferings, being conformed to His death.

(Philippians 3:10)

Now I truly loved the Lord and had given Him my heart and my life and wanted nothing more than to bring Him joy. But, in the midst of so much service for Him, I sometimes lost sight of the importance of just being His child.

And so, I sat in my chair and asked God to renew my relationship with Him. I prayed that He would fill me with His contentment and peace as I found true joy in just belonging to Him. It was during those days and weeks that God showed me more of Himself than ever before, because I wasn't busy doing so much that I didn't have time to just get to know Him better and love Him more.

I began thinking about how my marriage would be if I just did things for my husband all the time but didn't spend quality time being with Him. Sometimes, when I'm cleaning the house or ironing or decorating...all in an effort to make our home special for my husband...he will ask me to just stop and come and sit with him. He likes having a neat home and good meals and clean clothes, but he wants time with me. He wants to know that I enjoy just being with him, listening to his heart and that I am totally content with him. That is such an important part of a good relationship.

And then, as I think of the eagle knowing not to go over oceans where there are no updrafts to carry him, I realize that I should be aware of what to avoid in my spiritual life. Maybe I'm facing a spiritually challenging time because of a difficult situation, so I need to avoid things that would cause discouragement or weariness. I need to be in the Word more, I need to be with people who encourage and uplift me, I need to get more rest than usual and I need to spend time in prayer, letting God carry my load. I also need to make sure that I'm getting plenty of nourishment from God's Word for the journey.

All scripture is inspired by God and is profitable for teaching, for reproof, for correction, for training in righteousness; that the man of God may be adequate, equipped for every good work.

(2 Timothy 3:16,17)

Sometimes now, in my busy schedule, I have to stop and ask, "Is this important to you Lord, or am I just wearing myself out flapping my wings?" You see, I'd always love to say yes to every invitation to speak, every woman who asks for counsel and every event where I can share God's love with others. But, that isn't always what God wants. And so, I've learned that I must remember the importance of spending time just "being" a beloved child of my Heavenly Father.

An important part of this is learning to delight in God and His Word.

Praise the Lord! How blessed is the man who fears the Lord, who greatly delights in His commandments.

(Psalm 112:1)

Now, I know what it means to delight in my children and grandchildren...but what does it mean to really delight in His commandments? I once read the following and it has stayed in my mind ever since:

D — Daily
E — everything
L — laid
I — into
G — God's
H — hands
T — triumphantly

I really, really like that. It means that I will find my joy and purpose in knowing my Savior and will therefore be able to daily lay everything into God's hands. . . triumphantly! Triumphantly means to celebrate the victory, and so as I leave my worries and problems in God's loving care, I can already rejoice in the victory He has planned for me. That is definitely using the updrafts to help me soar!

But thanks be to God, who gives us the victory through our Lord Jesus Christ.

(1 Corinthians 15:57)

NANA'S STORY

My little grandson came waddling into my room early in the morning. I was surprised that he had climbed out of the playpen in which he slept and wondered when he had learned to do that. As I picked him up he looked at me and said "Nana, mouse on!" He had such a concerned look on his face and my heart skipped a beat. At this age, he only put about three words together at a time, like "Nana, sit, pay (play)." I asked him again what he said and again he repeated with a deeply furrowed brow, "Nana, mouse on!" Oh no, I thought. Could a mouse have gotten into his playpen? Had he seen one scampering across the floor? We hadn't seen any since we'd moved into this house several years ago, but there was always a first time.

I told my husband what he said and quickly asked him to look for this little invader. It was horrible to think of a mouse near my precious grandchild, and I was eager to find the culprit. He searched and I searched, but we couldn't find any evidence of the little creature. All the time, I'm holding my grandson and he keeps repeating the same thing, "Mouse on, Nana!" He was getting more and more concerned each time he said it. I wanted so much to put him at ease and show him there was no mouse, but he didn't seem relieved. We looked everywhere, getting more and more frustrated that we couldn't find the source of his concern.

At last, after finding nothing, my husband took him into bed with him and I got up to start getting ready for the day. About 15 minutes later, I came out of the bathroom and went to pick up my grandson so that my husband could get dressed. As I walked towards him, he looked up at me and gave me a huge grin and said, "Yea Nana! Mouse on!" As he did this, he pointed to my mouth and I realized that I had put my mouth (lipstick) on! He had been so concerned that his Nana had no mouth (mouse) and was greatly relieved that I had finally put it back on! (Does that give you a clue as to how I look without my make-up on?)

Are you wondering how I'm going to use this as an illustration? Well, the problem was really quite simple. Nana's mouth had disappeared overnight and now had reappeared, so all was well in the world. A tube of lipstick was all that was needed. But, because we didn't understand, we worked ourselves into a frenzy trying to solve the problem. The simplicity of God's truth is so clear:

Delight yourself in the Lord; and He will give you the desires of your heart.

(Psalm 37:4)

RESTING

Stopping, sitting, slowing down
Just looking up and not around.

Unworried and unhurried thoughts
Enjoying peace which can't be bought.

Knowing that I am God's child
Keeping heart both pure and mild.

Leaving troubled thoughts behind
Letting Him control my mind.

Remembering I am forgiv'n
Knowing that I'm bound for heav'n.

Stopping, sitting, slowing down
Just looking up and not around.

Carol Hopson

CHAPTER 11

HANDLING CRITICISM WISELY

I really don't like criticism very much, do you? It's always hard to hear someone tell you that they don't like what you did or how you did it. I remember speaking at a women's retreat and having many, many women come and share with me how much God had used my messages in their lives. Hearts were changed, children were born into the kingdom, and yet...as I went to bed that night, that's not what my mind thought of. You see, one woman felt the need to come up afterwards and tell me that she didn't like something I'd said in my message. She was very hurtful, negative, and bitter. I knew her problem was with the Lord, but it still hurt and was discouraging, since I had put so much time and prayer into preparing for this retreat.

It's time to look at the eagle again. While living in the beautiful Northwest, my husband and I were out on a boating trip to the San Juan Islands. Being a student of eagles, I'm always looking for them in places like that and when I spotted one very near the shoreline, we pulled the boat as close as we could get. As I gazed up into the treetop, the magnificent bald eagle sat so proudly on the top branch of the barren tree. Suddenly, several black crows appeared out of nowhere and started crowing loudly at the eagle. When he didn't respond, they began darting at him, over and over, getting within inches of him each time. They continued to screech and taunt him for 10-15 minutes. I've learned that crows are notorious for this tactic and it almost always works for them. They are able to gang up on and intimidate most other birds and get their way. As I watched this, I kept waiting for the eagle to snap at them or try to get away from them but he did neither. He just ignored them and held his position...at the top of the tree. They finally gave up and flew away, probably in search of someone more vulnerable to their attacks. I was struck by how regal the eagle remained through all the taunting. He never gave up his position, never glanced their way, or withdrew from their continual, irritating attacks. He didn't change who he was because of who they were.

I clearly remember thinking "If only I could be more like that eagle!" And then the Lord seemed to be saying to me, "You can, with my help."

Be steadfast immovable, always abounding in the work of the Lord, knowing that your toil is not in vain in the Lord.

(1 Corinthians 15:58)

It all gets down to staying focused and not listening to the "pecking and crowing" that comes my way. Jesus said, *"My sheep hear my voice, and they know me and follow me."*

I only need to listen to my Shepherd's voice and submit to what He asks me to do. He is the only One I need to seek to please. I can be gracious to those who are critical or offensive as Colossians 3:12-17 teaches, but I don't need to dwell on what they say or attempt to please them. This takes the sting out of criticism. If you're continually being criticized by a mate, a relative, co-worker, or friend, take heart. You don't need to let it affect your joy.

Sometimes it's extremely difficult to be quiet when you're mistreated or falsely accused, but we can learn from Paul who said, *"None of these things move me"* (Acts 20:24 KJV). He did not say, "None of these things hurt me." It is okay to be hurt, but we don't need to be moved from who we are in Christ, by what others say, think or do.

God's Word says:

This I know, that God is for me. In God, whose word I praise, in the Lord, whose word I praise, In God I have put my trust, I shall not be afraid. What can man do to me?

(Psalm 56:9b-11)

We also know that there are times when we need to listen to criticism and humble ourselves and submit to it. I remember when someone I dearly loved shared that I had caused real pain in her life by something I had said or done. I was truly shocked and it didn't even make sense to me as I listened to the words, but they were very real to this person. I had to admit that what was said was true, even if I didn't remember it or think it. It was still a reality to someone I loved and trusted and so I needed to respond correctly.

My human heart wanted to defend myself and try to explain that I never thought that or felt that way. But, God's Word says we are to "humble ourselves" and I knew that was what I needed to do. I asked the person to get on her knees with me while I prayed and asked God for forgiveness for offending her. I wept out of great sadness for the pain I had unknowingly caused and then asked her for forgiveness. It was granted and the burden in my heart was lifted. It was still painful to think about at times and yet, I was so thankful that God had shown me that the correct response in this situation was total humility. Sometimes, we are blind to how we come across to others and God needs to work on us in painful ways to make us more like Himself. In the end, I could look back and see how God had honored my obedience. My relationship with that person was, and is, richer and sweeter than ever before.

How do we know the difference in these two types of criticism? First of all, look at the one who is making the accusations. Is this person seeking God's best for you? Is it someone you respect or trust? Secondly, ask God right away if there is any truth to this criticism. Be open and He will reveal it to you. Your two choices are to repent and ask forgiveness, or ignore it and not let it affect you or your ministry. God will always show you which is His will if you are open to accepting it.

Nana's Story

My daughter was having a deep conversation with her 5-year old son, Elliot. They were talking about what he could be when he grew up. Jennifer asked if he might like to be a teacher, or a fireman like his uncle. Elliot sat quietly and contemplated. His mother went on to assure him he could be a policeman or a doctor or whatever he chose to be. Like all young mothers, she was trying to inspire him and show her support of whatever he'd choose to be when he grew up.

Finally, after a long silence, Elliot looked up at his mother and said, "Mommy, do you think it would be okay if I just be me?" My daughter smiled and hugged him and understood his little heart completely. She then assured him that she loved him just the way he was! How I love this story as it illustrates God's love for us. Sometimes we think we need to be something special or important to please God. We look at others and think we should try to be like them or have big degrees or at least be able to teach a Bible Study like someone else. But God, our Father, says, "It's okay to just be you! I made you and I love you just the way you are!"

I will give thanks to Thee, for I am fearfully and wonderfully made; wonderful are Thy works, and my soul knows it very well.

(Psalm 139:14)

I'LL JUST BE ME

Sometimes we wish that we could be
Like someone else we know.
And look like them and act like them
And have our lives just so.

But that is not what God has planned
And not what pleases Him.
For He has made each one of us
And not just on a whim.

He planned each hair, each size and shape
And numbered all our days.
And His desire in all of this
Was that we'd bring Him praise.

So thank You, God, for making us
The way you thought 'twas best.
Please help us use our lives for You
So others will be blessed.

Carol Hopson

CHAPTER 12

STAYING FOCUSED WHEN TROUBLED

It seems to happen more often than not. Things are going along pretty well and then a crisis comes up. Maybe it's news from a doctor, or an upsetting phone call. Recently, I've had both and it always seems to come as a surprise, even though I know that the Scripture says not to be surprised by these things. (James 1:3-5) It's like a sudden sickness that attacks you in unexpected ways; life suddenly looks grim, burdens seem heavier and the days ahead loom dark and dreary. I've had those exact feelings when false rumors were started about my husband and me. I'm always amazed at how quickly Christians and others are open to listen to false reports and pass them on. I'm sure that I've been guilty also and for that I've had to ask forgiveness and seek God's control of my mind and my words.

What can we learn from the eagle during these times of physical sickness or emotional turmoil? An eagle is seldom sick because he is very careful about his daily diet. He will choose different foods, depending on his body's needs and unlike his cousin, the vulture, he will never eat rotten or decaying food. But when he is sick, he usually finds a high, secluded place and lays on his back with outspread wings. He then stays completely still and focuses his eyes on the sun until his strength has returned and he feels healthy and ready to soar again.

This incredible truth about eagles has impacted my life in very real ways. When I was desperately sick after surgery and the doctors couldn't find the cause of the infection that invaded my body, I was brought to a very low point. I couldn't eat or keep anything in my body for over 3 months and I knew my life was slipping away. Since I was in a new community, with brand new doctors, they didn't take ownership of my problem and I kept getting passed from one doctor to another as I'd appear again and again in the emergency room. As I laid in my bed day after day, week after week, the discouragement was overwhelming. Then, one morning, God reminded me of the eagle's source of healing. He pulls away from all distractions, opens himself up by lying on his back with outspread wings, and focuses on the source of his healing....the sun.

One day, when I was so discouraged and weak from having no food for weeks, God brought this story to my mind and He seemed to put it on my heart to do those three things. I felt that I needed to pull away from distractions and change my thought life. If I focused on my health, my hopelessness, or what I didn't have, then my heart would stay troubled and discouraged all day long. So, I needed to focus on the truths of God's Word and on hope, no matter what I was feeling inside. I also needed to open myself up to accept what God had planned for my life. It was very powerful to stretch out my arms and lie on my back, in my sickness, and say, "God, I trust You with my health and my life. Help me accept this and use it forYour glory. I surrender my desires and my body to You."

Finally, I needed to focus on Jesus, the Son, my source of strength. To do this, I consciously would dwell on the many blessings that I had in my life at this point, such as my family, my wonderful Godly husband, the many years of ministry that God had given to me, the future hope of spending eternity with my Savior and so much more.

Hebrews 12:1-3 says:

...fixing our eyes on Jesus, the Author and Perfecter of our faith, Who, for the joy set before Him, endured the cross, despising the shame and has sat down at the right hand of God. For consider Him who has endured such hostility by sinners against Himself, so that you may not grow weary and lose heart.

As I chose to focus on the "Son" instead of self, I began to have hope again. God would eventually bring a doctor into my life who was determined to find the cure and she did just that over several months. The days and nights were often long, as I awaited God's timing, but my attitude changed because of my focus and those months in bed became times of spiritual growth, intercessory prayer and plans for future seminars on discouragement.

Are you facing some troubles today? Have you been discouraged for a long time because you don't feel like God is working and so you've lost your hope? Do you need a new focus and renewed hope? Then get alone with God, away from distractions, and open yourself up to Him. Surrender your deepest fears to Him and then trust Him enough to take care of you.

I love you Lord; you are my strength. The Lord is my Rock, my fortress, and my savior; my God is my rock, in whom I find protection. He is my shield, the strength of my salvation and my stronghold.
(Psalm 18:1,2 NLT)

The Lord is near to the brokenhearted, and saves those who are crushed in spirit.
(Psalm 34:18)

Let's take a look at David's struggle and situation as he wrote the eighteenth Psalm.

The ropes of death surrounded me, the floods of destruction swept over me. The grave wrapped its ropes around me; death itself stared me in the face. But in my distress I cried out to the Lord; yes, I prayed to my God for help. He heard me from his sanctuary; my cry reached his ears.
(Psalm 18:4-6 NLT)

By the end of his conversation with God, we see David's renewed heart:

As for God, his way is perfect. All the Lord's promises prove true. He is a shield for all who look to him for protection.
(Psalm 18:30 NLT)

You can see how distressed and hopeless David felt in verse four. But, we then see how he opened up his heart and will to the Lord and God met his need. The statement that strikes me the most is "As for God, his way is perfect." David's situation had not changed and I'm sure he didn't know how it was all going to turn out. But, he showed his complete submission to God with those words. My heart has rested only when I've been able to say...as for God His way is perfect...and truly mean it. It's always a choice!

NANA'S STORY

Monica was coming for a visit. She was my first and only grandchild at the time, and was about 20 months old. I couldn't wait! In conversations before their visit, my son mentioned that they didn't want me to pick up everything around the house that Monica shouldn't touch. They wanted me to leave things as they were so they could teach her to make "good choices" and not touch things. I had seen them talk to her many times about this. They would say, "Monica, are you going to make a good choice or a bad choice?" and then they would explain the difference.

When they arrived, they took her around the house and showed her the things she wasn't to touch. This was hard on Nana, but I wanted to totally support my children's efforts in training their daughter. Later that day, I couldn't find Monica so I began looking in all the rooms. I found her in my bedroom peering at a little figurine which was eye-level on my dresser. The door was almost closed so I just watched through the crack in the door. Monica looked around to see if anyone was watching and then reached her little hand up to touch it. She got her hand so close but then jerked it back and looked around again. She tried again but didn't make contact. Then she tried it with one finger but never touched the "forbidden" fruit. After four attempts, and without ever actually touching the figurine, she turned her little body around, shrugged her little shoulders and said firmly, "Good girl!" She then walked back out the door.

What an amazing sight to see a child so young make such a good choice when no one was looking. It was a picture that I have kept in my mind ever since as I've desired to make "good choices" that please my Heavenly Father. When I do this, I picture my heavenly Father saying, "Good girl, Carol!"

WELL DONE, MY PRECIOUS CHILD

I'd like to hear my Savior say
"Well done, my precious child!"
I'd like to know I'm pleasing Him
And bringing Him a smile.

I know He loves me as I am
And forgives me when I fall
And I'm so glad He knows my heart
And hears my every call.

But just because I love Him so,
At my life's setting sun
I'd love to hear those precious words
"Dear child of mine, well done!"

Carol Hopson

CHAPTER 13

BUILDING A STRONG HOME

I just received a phone call yesterday from someone whose home had truly fallen apart. There was so much heartache in this woman's voice and it was so painful to listen to her. She wondered why her husband was leaving her, why her unmarried daughter was pregnant and why her son was hanging out with troubled teens. Of course, I couldn't determine all the reasons behind these events, but as I listened to her story, it was evident that they had not been doing any "foundation building" in their home. They claimed to be a Christian family and yet they had let their home fall apart...piece by piece.

Before I go on, let me tell you what kind of foundation building the eagles do. It seems that they are very serious about mating and about building a strong, safe home for their little family. They will use the same nest for decades and so are determined to keep it strong and secure. They will work on strengthening or refurbishing it at least once a year, and sometimes more often than that. This process becomes intense in the winter as the weather seeks to tear apart their secure home. However, they want to make sure that they will always have a safe place to lay their eggs and raise their family, and so they are committed to the rebuilding process each year.

An eagle's nest will begin at maybe five feet in diameter and will stand about two feet tall. Over the years, their nest can expand to eight to twelve feet in diameter and will reach up to twenty feet tall! The weight of the nest can vary from one to two tons. As their life together grows, so their nest grows and becomes stronger and more secure. They don't allow a year to go by without strengthening their "home."

Isn't it amazing that we humans, created in the image of God, often don't seem to realize the importance of strengthening our homes! As the eagle knows the danger of allowing the outside forces to tear apart his nest, we should be even more aware of the worldly pressures, which seek to destroy our homes.

> *Don't become so well-adjusted to your culture that you fit into it without even thinking. Instead, fix your attention on God. You'll be changed from the inside out. Readily recognize what he wants from you and quickly respond to it. Unlike the culture around you, always dragging you down to its level of immaturity, God brings the best out of you, develops well-formed maturity in you.*
>
> (Romans 12:1,2 The Message)

God's Word not only warns us about the culture around us, but commands us to keep our families secure by making sure our family structure is Biblical and strong.

Children, obey your parents because you belong to the Lord, for this is the right thing to do. Honor your father and mother.

(Ephesians 4:1 NLT)

Now, if you think that children are born with a sweet, obedient spirit and are just eager to obey and honor their parents, you've probably never had children! On the contrary, all parents know that children need to be taught to obey their parents. I see this command as equally important for parents as for children. How can children learn to obey if their parents don't require obedience? I've observed this devastating behavior by parents hundreds of times. They give a command to a child and the child cries or defies them and the parent does nothing except look frustrated. Sometimes, the parent will raise his or her voice to make an impact, but the child knows there will be no other consequence and so he continues with his self-centered ways. We, as parents, are being disobedient to God's Word when we don't discipline and disciple our children from the earliest ages, to respect and honor their parents. This allows for the breakdown of our homes.

The passage goes on to state that fathers should not:

...make your children angry by the way you treat them. Rather, bring them up with the discipline and instruction approved by the Lord.

(Ephesians 6:4 NLT)

Can you imagine how different our Christian homes would be if all fathers regularly and lovingly instructed their children in the ways of the Lord? It seems that this is usually left up to the mother, when she has time, and it's no wonder that our homes are falling apart. We haven't followed the Biblical pattern for strong homes.

After listening to the heart-broken mother for awhile, I asked how involved her husband was with the training of their children. She related to me a familiar story, one I've heard too many times. "Well, he started out doing fairly well when they were really little, but gradually, his work took more time and he was tired when he got home, so I took on more and more. He really isn't involved at all in their discipline or their spiritual growth now. I've grown tired of doing it all and so haven't been as faithful as I should be." With hindsight, it's easy to see why this family fell apart. There was no renewal, no strengthening, no teamwork, and no continuing effort to stay committed to God's principles.

Another area of homebuilding mentioned in Ephesians 5:21-30 is the husband-wife relationship. This certainly had broken down in this marriage. God specifically tells us that we are to submit to one another and wives are to be subject to their husbands. Husbands are to be the leaders of the home and must love their wives with the same love that Christ showed to the church. Husbands are even told to love their wives as they love their own bodies. I asked the woman about her relationship with her husband and she told me that she felt unloved and taken for granted for many years but had done nothing about it. There had been no effort in recent years to strengthen their marriage or to seek help for their problems. They simply let life's pressures and Satan's attacks pull them farther apart and now their "nest" was truly falling apart.

This tragic situation reminded me of the importance of continually strengthening our homes and marriages. We need to make sure that we are checking our foundation for cracks, checking our hearts to make sure they are right with the Lord, checking to make sure we are requiring obedience from our children and checking to make sure that our love relationship with our mate is growing stronger every year.

My husband and I are going to celebrate our fortieth anniversary in a few months and we are often asked, "How have you stayed together for so long?" The answer is twofold: On our wedding day, we both committed to keep our relationship with the Lord first in our lives and then we promised to stay with each other for life, to grow together and serve our Lord together in whatever way He chose. Secondly, as we've sought to live according to God's plan for our marriage and family, He has blessed us beyond measure by increasing our love forty-fold. Don't get me wrong here...our marriage isn't perfect and we are definitely not perfect, we are human! We've had many struggles, hurts, changed plans, and discouragements, just like you have. But, as we've put each situation in God's hands and tried to be faithful to what His Word teaches, we have simply experienced God's grace and sufficiency every time. We would have failed in our own strength, but He is truly the great "Home-builder" and His principles never fail.

NANA'S STORY

My children related a story to me that I will never forget. Their child was having difficulty sleeping and was not behaving the way she usually did. They were parents who disciplined promptly and lovingly, but something had changed and they couldn't figure out why she was acting this way. After asking God for wisdom and researching some Christian books, they decided that possibly their child was feeling insecure because the dad had been busier than usual and wasn't seen hugging and cuddling his wife on the sofa in the evening. They decided to make a conscious effort to do this for about 15-20 minutes each night before putting their child to bed. Within two nights, the child was having no trouble sleeping and had returned to her obedient, loving nature. You see, the love of the parents gave this child the secure feeling that all was well at home. This happened years ago and those parents have never forgotten the lesson they learned. They continue to show affection and respect for each other in a way that has given their children a beautiful, secure "nest" in which to grow and develop. I once read a powerful statement that has stayed with me for many years. It simply said "One of the greatest gifts a father can give to his children is to love their mother."

Do you need to do some "nest building?" You can start right now by seeking God's wisdom and direction for your family. In Psalm 32:8 He promises,

I will instruct you and teach you in the way you should go. I will counsel you with my eye on you.

HOME SHOULD BE

Home should be a place where love
Is freely scattered 'round,
Where dreams can grow and flourish
And helpful words abound.

Home should be a place where time
Is spent to teach and train
Where parents strive to model what
They want their kids to attain.

Home should be a place where God
Is central to all plans
Where His Word is the authority
For anything at hand.

Home should be a place where hearts
Are strengthened day by day
Where God has fertile soil to plant
His seeds along the way.

Carol Hopson

FROM THE AUTHOR

There's one more story I'd like to share with you in closing. It's from the wonderful devotional book entitled *"Streams in the Desert"* by L. B. Cowman.

One day in autumn, while on the open prairie, I saw an eagle mortally wounded by a rifle shot. With his eyes still gleaming like small circles of light, he slowly turned his head, giving one last searching and longing look toward the sky. He had often swept those starry spaces with his wonderful wings. The beautiful sky was the home of his heart. It was the eagle's domain. It was there he had displayed his

splendid strength a thousand times. In those lofty heights, he had played with the lightning, and raced the wind. And now, far below his home, the eagle lay dying. He faced death because...just once...he forgot and flew too low.
My soul is that eagle. This is not its home. It must never lose its skyward look, I must keep faith, I must keep hope, I must keep courage, I must keep Christ. There is no time for my soul to retreat. Keep your skyward look, my soul; keep your skyward look!

Praise God that we are not mortally wounded when we give in to the storms of life. God is always ready to forgive us, strengthen us, and bring us closer to Himself. However, I love this picture of continually looking upward where all our hope and joy is found.

I do pray that this book will help you rise above the storms of life as you allow the currents of God's Word and the knowledge of His love to lift you to new heights. And so, as you trust God's truths, remember that God is always there to help you "mount up with wings as eagles" to where you can clearly see the " Son."

KEEP YOUR SKYWARD LOOK, MY SOUL

Keep your skyward look, my soul
There's nothing down below
Except some fears and heartaches
And worries that will grow.

Keep your skyward look, my soul
It's what God wants for me
For as I stay above the storm
His precious truths I'll see.

Keep your skyward look, my soul
He's all I need and more
For I have found no joy without
This Savior I adore.

Carol Hopson

ACKNOWLEDGEMENTS

I gratefully acknowledge the incredible work of Kenneth Price in his book *"The Eagle Christian"* published by *Old Faithful Publishing Co.*, Wetumpka, Alabama; Copyright 1984.

Other sources used:

Charles Preston

Golden Eagle, Sovereign of the Skies, Graphic Arts Center Publishing; Copyright 1993

Doug Storer

Encyclopedia of Amazing but True Facts, Sterling Publishing Co., New York, NY; Copyright 1980

Institute in Basic Youth Conflicts, Inc.

Character Sketches, from the pages of *Scripture, Rand McNally and Company Publishers*; Copyright 1976

Derek Hall

Encyclopedia of North American Birds

Thunder Bay Press, San Diego, California; Copyright 2004

The New Encyclopedia Britannica: *William Benton Publishers*, Chicago, Illinois; Copyright 1984